Top 30 Most D

Empanada Recipes

An Empanada Cookbook

by Graham Bourdain

Copyright © 2023 Graham Bourdain

All Rights Reserved

Disclaimer

Reasonable care has been taken to ensure that the information presented in this ebook is accurate. However, the reader should understand that the information provided does not constitute legal, medical or professional advice of any kind.

No Liability: this product is supplied "as is" and without warranties. All warranties, express or implied, are hereby disclaimed. Use of this product constitutes acceptance of the "No Liability" policy. If you do not agree with this policy, you are not permitted to use or distribute this product.

We shall not be liable for any losses or damages whatsoever

(including, without limitation, consequential loss or damage) directly or indirectly arising from the use of this product.

Please note that the nutritional values may vary depending on the specific ingredients and measurements used, as well as the method of cooking.

It's always a good idea to consult a registered dietitian or use an online nutrition calculator to get the most accurate nutritional value for a recipe, based on the ingredients and measurements you use.

Table of Contents

1. Chicken and Broccoli Empanadas

Prep: 20 min. Cook: 20 min. Ready In: 40 min. Servings: 4

Ingredients:

1-pound boneless, skinless chicken breasts, diced

1/2 cup diced onion

1/2 cup diced red bell pepper

1/4 cup diced jalapeno pepper

1 cup chopped broccoli florets

1/4 teaspoon cayenne pepper

1/4 teaspoon black pepper

1/4 teaspoon salt

1/4 cup grated cheddar cheese

1/4 cup grated Monterey Jack cheese

1 package (15 oz) store-bought empanada dough

1 large egg, beaten with 1 tablespoon water

Cooking Directions:

Alright folks, get ready for a treat, these Chicken and Broccoli Empanadas are going to be a hit.

First things first, preheat your oven to 375 degrees F. Next, heat a skillet over medium-high heat and cook the chicken until browned, about 5 minutes. Remove the chicken from the skillet with a slotted spoon and set it aside. Add the onion, red bell pepper, jalapeno pepper and broccoli to the skillet, and cook until softened, about 5 minutes. Stir in the cayenne pepper, black pepper, and salt. Cook for another minute. Stir in the chicken, cheddar cheese and Monterey Jack cheese into the skillet, cook until cheese melted.

Now it's time to assemble the empanadas. Roll out the empanada dough on a lightly floured surface to about 1/8-inch thickness. Cut the dough into 4-inch circles using a round cookie cutter or the rim of a glass. Spoon about 2 tablespoons of the chicken and broccoli filling onto one half of each dough circle, leaving a 1/2-inch border around the edges. Brush the beaten egg around the edges of the dough, then fold the dough over the filling to form a half-moon shape. Press the edges together to seal.

Place the empanadas on a baking sheet and brush the tops with the remaining beaten egg. Bake for 20 minutes, or until golden brown.

Serve hot, garnished with fresh chopped parsley, or with a spicy salsa on the side. And don't forget a cold beer because these empanadas are going to be a hit.

Enjoy

2. Beef and Onion Empanadas

Prep: 20 min. Cook: 20 min. Ready In: 40 min. Servings: 4

Ingredients:

1 pound ground beef

1/2 cup diced onion

1/4 teaspoon cumin

1/4 teaspoon smoked paprika

1/4 teaspoon black pepper

1/4 teaspoon salt

1/4 cup grated cheddar cheese

1/4 cup grated Monterey Jack cheese

1 package (15 oz) store-bought empanada dough

1 large egg, beaten with 1 tablespoon water

Cooking Directions:

Alright folks, get ready for a delicious treat with these Beef and Onion Empanadas.

First things first, preheat your oven to 375 degrees F. Next, heat a skillet over medium-high heat and cook the beef until browned, about 5 minutes. Remove the beef from the skillet with a slotted spoon and set it aside. Add the diced onion to the skillet, and cook until softened, about 5 minutes. Stir in the cumin, smoked paprika, black pepper, and salt. Cook for another minute. Stir in the beef, cheddar cheese and Monterey Jack cheese into the skillet, cook until cheese melted.

Now it's time to assemble the empanadas. Roll out the empanada dough on a lightly floured surface to about 1/8-inch thickness. Cut the dough into 4-inch circles using a round cookie cutter or the rim of a glass.

Spoon about 2 tablespoons of the beef and onion filling onto one half of each dough circle, leaving a 1/2-inch border around the edges. Brush the beaten egg around the edges of the dough, then fold the dough over the filling to form a half-moon shape. Press the edges together to seal.

Place the empanadas on a baking sheet and brush the tops with the remaining beaten egg. Bake for 20 minutes, or until golden brown.

Serve hot, garnished with fresh chopped parsley, or with a spicy salsa on the side. And don't forget a cold beer because these empanadas are going to be a hit.

Enjoy

3. Black Bean and Corn Empanadas

Prep: 20 min. Cook: 20 min. Ready In: 40 min. Servings: 4

Ingredients:

1 can black beans, drained and rinsed

1/2 cup frozen corn

1/4 cup diced onion

1/4 cup diced red bell pepper

1/4 teaspoon cumin

1/4 teaspoon smoked paprika

1/4 teaspoon black pepper

1/4 teaspoon salt

1/4 cup grated cheddar cheese

1/4 cup grated Monterey Jack cheese

1 package (15 oz) store-bought empanada dough

1 large egg, beaten with 1 tablespoon water

Cooking Directions:

Alright folks, if you're looking for a delicious and hearty empanada recipe that's a little out of the ordinary, then look no further than these Black Bean and Corn Empanadas.

First, we're going to preheat that oven to 375 degrees F. In a skillet, sauté diced onion and red bell pepper until softened, about 5 minutes. Next, add in a can of drained and rinsed black beans, 1/2 cup of frozen corn, cumin, smoked paprika, black pepper, and salt. Cook for another 2-3 minutes, until everything is heated through. Now, it's time to add some cheese. Stir in the cheddar cheese and Monterey Jack cheese until melted. Now it's time to assemble the empanadas. Roll out the empanada dough on a lightly floured surface to about 1/8-inch thickness. Cut the dough into 4-inch circles using a round cookie cutter or the rim of a glass. Spoon about 2 tablespoons of the black bean and corn filling onto one half of each dough circle, leaving a 1/2-inch border around the edges. Brush the beaten egg around the edges of the dough, then fold the dough over the filling to form a half-moon shape. Press the edges together to seal.

Place the empanadas on a baking sheet and brush the tops with the remaining beaten egg. Pop those bad boys in the oven and bake for 20 minutes, or until golden brown.

Serve hot, garnished with fresh chopped cilantro, or with a spicy salsa on the side. And don't forget a cold beer because these empanadas are going to be a crowd pleaser.

Enjoy

4. Salmon and Capers Empanadas

Prep: 15 min. Cook: 30 min. Ready In: 45 min. Servings: 4

Ingredients:

1-pound cooked salmon, flaked

1/4 cup diced onion

1/4 cup diced red bell pepper

1/4 cup diced green bell pepper

1/4 cup diced yellow bell pepper

1/4 teaspoon black pepper

1/4 teaspoon salt

1/4 cup capers

1/4 cup grated cheddar cheese

1/4 cup grated Monterey Jack cheese

1 package (15 oz) store-bought empanada dough

1 large egg, beaten with 1 tablespoon water

Cooking Directions:

Get ready for a culinary journey with these Salmon and Capers Empanadas. A unique combination of flavors that will transport you to a different place with every bite. Trust me, this recipe is worth trying. Let's get cooking!

First, preheat that oven to 375 degrees F. In a skillet, sauté diced onion, red bell pepper, green bell pepper, and yellow bell pepper until softened, about 5 minutes. Next, add in the flaked salmon, black pepper, salt, and capers. Cook for another 2-3 minutes, until everything is heated through. Now, it's time to add some cheese. Stir in the cheddar cheese and Monterey Jack cheese until melted.

Now it's time to assemble the empanadas. Roll out the empanada dough on a lightly floured surface to about 1/8-inch thickness. Cut the dough into 4-inch circles using a round cookie cutter or the rim of a glass. Spoon about 2 tablespoons of the salmon and capers filling onto one half of each dough circle, leaving a 1/2-inch border around the edges. Brush the beaten egg around the edges of the dough, then fold the dough over the filling to form a half-moon shape. Press the edges together to seal. Place the empanadas on a baking sheet and brush the tops with the remaining beaten egg. Pop those bad boys in the oven and bake for 20 minutes, or until golden brown.

Serve hot, garnished with fresh chopped parsley, or with a lemony aioli on the side. And don't forget a cold beer because these empanadas are going to be a hit.

Enjoy

5. Shrimp and Tomato Empanadas

Prep: 20 min. Cook: 20 min. Ready In: 40 min. Servings: 4

Ingredients:

1 pound of raw shrimp, peeled and deveined

1/2 cup diced onion

2 cloves of minced garlic

1/2 cup diced tomatoes

1/4 cup chopped cilantro

1/2 teaspoon smoked paprika

1/4 teaspoon cumin

Salt and pepper to taste

1 egg, beaten

Store-bought empanada dough

Cooking Directions:

Listen up folks, you want a taste of something truly special? These shrimp and tomato empanadas are where it's at. Trust me, I've traveled the world and I know my empanadas. So, fire up the stove and let's get cooking.

In a skillet, heat the olive oil over medium heat. Add the onion and garlic and cook until softened, about 5 minutes.

Add the shrimp and cook until they turn pink, about 3 minutes.

Stir in the diced tomatoes, cumin, smoked paprika, and salt. Cook for an additional 5 minutes, or until the mixture has thickened.

Remove from heat and stir in the chopped cilantro.

Preheat the oven to 375°F.

Roll out the empanada dough on a lightly floured surface.

Cut the dough into 4-inch circles.

Place about 2 tablespoons of the shrimp mixture on one half of each circle. Brush the edges with the beaten egg.

Fold the dough over the filling to form a half-moon shape and press the edges with a fork to seal.

Brush the top with the beaten egg.

Place the empanadas on a baking sheet and bake for about 20 minutes, or until golden brown.

Alright, the timer just went off and these bad boys are looking beautiful. Crispy on the outside, hot, and juicy on the inside. Perfection. Serve them up with a cold beer and enjoy. Bon appétit!

Enjoy

6. Tuna and Red Onion Empanadas

Prep: 15 min. Cook: 20 min. Ready In: 35 min. Servings: 4

Ingredients:

1 package store-bought empanada dough

1 can of tuna, drained

1/2 red onion, finely diced

1/4 cup chopped fresh cilantro

1/4 cup raisins

1/4 cup sliced green olives

1/4 teaspoon cumin

Salt and pepper

1 egg, beaten

Cooking Directions:

Empanadas, those delicious little pockets of heaven filled with all sorts of goodies. Today, we're going to be making something special, Tuna and Red Onion Empanadas. Perfect for a quick lunch or a snack, these babies are packed with flavor and easy to make. So, let's get started.

Preheat the oven to 375 degrees F (190 degrees C). Line a baking sheet with parchment paper.

Dust a clean surface with flour and roll out the empanada dough to 1/8-inch thickness.

In a medium bowl, combine the tuna, red onion, cilantro, raisins, olives, cumin, salt, and pepper.

Place a heaping tablespoon of the filling onto one half of each round of dough, leaving a 1/2-inch border around the edges.

Brush the edges of the dough with the beaten egg, then fold the dough over the filling and press the edges to seal.

Place the empanadas on the prepared baking sheet and brush the tops with the remaining egg.

Bake for 20 minutes, or until golden brown.

And there you have it folks, Tuna, and Red Onion Empanadas. These little pockets of deliciousness are perfect for any occasion, whether it's a quick lunch or a snack. So, go ahead and give them a try, and let me know what you think. Bon Appetit!

Enjoy

7. Egg and Bacon Empanadas

Prep: 15 min. Cook: 20 min. Ready In: 35 min. Servings: 4

Ingredients:

All-purpose flour for dusting

1 package store-bought empanada dough

4 eggs

4 slices of bacon, cooked and diced

1/4 cup diced onion

1/4 cup diced bell pepper

1/4 cup diced jalapeño pepper

1/4 cup shredded cheddar cheese

Salt and pepper

1 egg, beaten

Cooking Directions:

Empanadas, the ultimate comfort food. And today, we're going to be making something that's going to knock your socks off, Egg and Bacon Empanadas. These bad boys are packed with flavor and perfect for a lazy brunch or a satisfying snack. So, let's get cracking.

Preheat the oven to 375 degrees F (190 degrees C). Line a baking sheet with parchment paper. Dust a clean surface with flour and roll out the empanada dough to 1/8-inch thickness. In a medium skillet, scramble the eggs until cooked through. In a medium bowl, combine the scrambled eggs, bacon, onion, bell pepper, jalapeño pepper, cheddar cheese, salt, and pepper.

Place a heaping tablespoon of the filling onto one half of each round of dough, leaving a 1/2-inch border around the edges.

Brush the edges of the dough with the beaten egg, then fold the dough over the filling and press the edges to seal.

Place the empanadas on the prepared baking sheet and brush the tops with the remaining egg.

Bake for 20 minutes, or until golden brown.

And there you have it folks, Egg and Bacon Empanadas. Perfect for a lazy brunch or a satisfying snack, these babies are sure to please. So, go ahead and give them a try, and let me know what you think. Bon Appetit!

Enjoy

8. Turkey and Gravy Empanadas

Prep: 15 min. Cook: 30 min. Ready In: 45 min. Servings: 4

Ingredients:

All-purpose flour for dusting

1 package store-bought empanada dough

2 cups cooked turkey, diced

1/4 cup diced onion

1/4 cup diced celery

1/4 cup diced carrots

1/4 cup turkey gravy

Salt and pepper

1 egg, beaten

Cooking Directions:

Empanadas, the ultimate way to use up leftovers. And today, we're going to be making something that's going to make your Thanksgiving leftovers sing, Turkey and Gravy Empanadas. These bad boys are packed with flavor and perfect for a quick lunch or a snack. So, let's get started.

Preheat the oven to 375 degrees F (190 degrees C). Line a baking sheet with parchment paper.

Dust a clean surface with flour and roll out the empanada dough to 1/8-inch thickness.

In a medium bowl, combine the turkey, onion, celery, carrots, gravy, salt, and pepper.

Place a heaping tablespoon of the filling onto one half of each round of dough, leaving a 1/2-inch border around the edges.

Brush the edges of the dough with the beaten egg, then fold the dough over the filling and press the edges to seal.

Place the empanadas on the prepared baking sheet and brush the tops with the remaining egg.

Bake for 20 minutes, or until golden brown.

And there you have it folks, Turkey and Gravy Empanadas. These little pockets of deliciousness are the perfect way to use up those Thanksgiving leftovers. So, go ahead and give them a try, and let me know what you think. Bon Appetit!

Enjoy

9. Chicken and Cauliflower Empanadas

Prep: 15 min. Cook: 20 min. Ready In: 35 min. Servings: 4

Ingredients:

All-purpose flour for dusting

1 package store-bought empanada dough

2 cups cooked chicken, diced

1 cup cooked and mashed cauliflower

1/4 cup diced onion

1/4 cup diced bell pepper

1/4 cup diced jalapeño pepper

1/4 cup shredded cheddar cheese

Salt and pepper

1 egg, beaten

Cooking Directions:

Empanadas, a true global dish, adaptable to any flavor and ingredients. Today, we're going to be making something special, Chicken and Cauliflower Empanadas. Perfect for a quick lunch or a snack, these babies are packed with flavor and easy to make. So, let's get started.

Preheat the oven to 375 degrees F (190 degrees C). Line a baking sheet with parchment paper.

Dust a clean surface with flour and roll out the empanada dough to 1/8-inch thickness.

In a medium bowl, combine the chicken, mashed cauliflower, onion, bell pepper, jalapeño pepper, cheddar cheese, salt, and pepper.

Place a heaping tablespoon of the filling onto one half of each round of dough, leaving a 1/2-inch border around the edges.

Brush the edges of the dough with the beaten egg, then fold the dough over the filling and press the edges to seal.

Place the empanadas on the prepared baking sheet and brush the tops with the remaining egg.

Bake for 20 minutes, or until golden brown.

And there you have it folks, Chicken and Cauliflower Empanadas. These little pockets of deliciousness are perfect for any occasion, whether it's a quick lunch or a snack. So, go ahead and give them a try, and let me know what you think. Bon Appetit!

Enjoy

10. Beef and Carrot Empanadas

Prep: 30 min. Cook: 30 min. Ready In: 1 h. Servings: 4

Ingredients:

1 lb. beef chuck, cut into small cubes

1 onion, diced

3 cloves of garlic, minced

1 cup of grated carrots

1 teaspoon of paprika

1 teaspoon of cumin

1 teaspoon of salt

1/2 teaspoon of black pepper

1/2 teaspoon of dried oregano

1/4 cup of raisins

1/4 cup of green olives, sliced

1 package of store-bought empanada dough

1 egg, beaten

Cooking Directions:

Empanadas, my friends, are the ultimate street food. They're portable, delicious, and can be filled with just about anything. Today, we're going to show you how to make beef and carrot empanadas that will blow your mind. Trust me, these bad boys are worth the effort.

In a large skillet, brown the beef over medium-high heat until it's cooked through. Drain any excess fat. Add the onion and garlic to the skillet and cook until softened, about 5 minutes. Stir in the grated carrots, paprika, cumin, salt, black pepper, and oregano. Cook for an additional 5 minutes. Stir in the raisins and green olives and cook for a final 2 minutes. Remove from heat and let cool. Preheat the oven to 375 degrees F (190 degrees C). Roll out the store-bought empanada dough on a lightly floured surface. Cut into circles using a cookie cutter or a glass. Place a spoonful of the beef and carrot mixture on one half of each empanada dough circle. Brush the edges of the dough with the beaten egg. Fold the dough over the filling to create a half-moon shape and press the edges together to seal. Place the empanadas on a baking sheet and brush the tops with the remaining beaten egg.

Bake for 20-25 minutes, or until golden brown.

And there you have it, folks. Beef and carrot empanadas that will make your taste buds dance. Serve them up with some chimichurri or aioli and enjoy. Trust me, these are the real deal. Buen provecho!

Enjoy

11. Pork and Apricot Empanadas

Prep: 45 min. Cook: 30 min. Ready In: 1 h. 15 min. Servings: 4

Ingredients:

1 lb. pork shoulder, cut into small cubes

1 onion, diced

3 cloves of garlic, minced

1 cup of diced apricots

1 teaspoon of smoked paprika

1 teaspoon of cumin

1 teaspoon of salt

1/2 teaspoon of black pepper

1/4 cup of slivered almonds

1/4 cup of green olives, sliced

1/4 cup of cilantro, chopped

1 package of store-bought empanada dough

1 egg, beaten

Cooking Directions:

Empanadas, my dear friends, are the ultimate comfort food. They're warm, flaky and can be filled with just about anything. Today, we're going to show you how to make pork and apricot empanadas that will change the way you think about empanadas. Trust me, these are not your grandma's empanadas.

In a large skillet, brown the pork over medium-high heat until it's cooked through. Drain any excess fat.

Add the onion and garlic to the skillet and cook until softened, about 5 minutes. Stir in the diced apricots, smoked paprika, cumin, salt, and black pepper. Cook for an additional 5 minutes. Stir in the slivered almonds, green olives, and cilantro. Cook for a final 2 minutes. Remove from heat and let cool. Preheat the oven to 375 degrees F (190 degrees C). Roll out the store-bought empanada dough on a lightly floured surface. Cut into circles using a cookie cutter or a glass.

Place a spoonful of the pork and apricot mixture on one half of each empanada dough circle. Brush the edges of the dough with the beaten egg. Fold the dough over the filling to create a half-moon shape and press the edges together to seal. Place the empanadas on a baking sheet and brush the tops with the remaining beaten egg.

Bake for 20-25 minutes, or until golden brown.

And there you have it, folks. Pork and apricot empanadas that will make your taste buds sing. Serve them up with some chimichurri or aioli and enjoy. Trust me, these are the real deal. Buen provecho!

Enjoy

12. Black Bean and Avocado Empanadas

Prep: 30 min. Cook: 20 min. Ready In: 50 min. Servings: 4

Ingredients:

1 can of black beans, drained and rinsed

1/2 onion, diced

3 cloves of garlic, minced

1 avocado, diced

1 teaspoon of cumin

1/2 teaspoon of chili powder

1/2 teaspoon of salt

1/4 teaspoon of black pepper

1/4 cup of cilantro, chopped

1 package of store-bought empanada dough

1 egg, beaten

Cooking Directions:

Empanadas, my friends, are the epitome of versatile. They can be filled with just about anything and today we're going to show you how to make some Black Bean and Avocado Empanadas that will knock your socks off. These empanadas are not only delicious but also vegetarian and gluten-free, so you can enjoy them with no guilt, and no judgement.

In a medium skillet, sauté the onion and garlic over medium heat until softened, about 5 minutes. Stir in the black beans, avocado, cumin, chili powder, salt, and black pepper. Cook for an additional 5 minutes.

Stir in the cilantro. Cook for a final 2 minutes. Remove from heat and let cool. Preheat the oven to 375 degrees F (190 degrees C). Roll out the store-bought empanada dough on a lightly floured surface. Cut into circles using a cookie cutter or a glass. Place a spoonful of the black bean and avocado mixture on one half of each empanada dough circle. Brush the edges of the dough with the beaten egg. Fold the dough over the filling to create a half-moon shape and press the edges together to seal. Place the empanadas on a baking sheet and brush the tops with the remaining beaten egg. Bake for 15-20 minutes, or until golden brown.

And there you have it, folks. Black Bean and Avocado Empanadas that will make your taste buds dance. Serve them up with some salsa or guacamole and enjoy. Trust me, these are the real deal. Buen provecho!

Enjoy

13. Salmon and Lemon Empanadas

Prep: 30 min. Cook: 20 min. Ready In: 50 min. Servings: 4

Ingredients:

1 lb. of fresh salmon fillet, skin removed and flaked

1/2 onion, diced

1/2 cup of diced red bell pepper

1/4 cup of lemon juice

1/4 cup of parsley, chopped

1 teaspoon of salt

1/4 teaspoon of black pepper

1/4 cup of grated parmesan cheese

1 package of store-bought empanada dough

1 egg, beaten

Cooking Directions:

Empanadas, my dear friends, are the ultimate party food. They're easy to make, easy to eat, and can be filled with just about anything. Today, we're going to show you how to make some Salmon and Lemon Empanadas that will make your guests ask for seconds, and maybe even thirds. Trust me, these empanadas are something special.

In a medium skillet, sauté the onion and red bell pepper over medium heat until softened, about 5 minutes. Stir in the flaked salmon, lemon juice, parsley, salt, and black pepper. Cook for an additional 2 minutes.

Stir in the parmesan cheese. Cook for a final 1 minute. Remove from heat and let cool. Preheat the oven to 375 degrees F (190 degrees C).

Roll out the store-bought empanada dough on a lightly floured surface. Cut into circles using a cookie cutter or a glass. Place a spoonful of the salmon and lemon mixture on one half of each empanada dough circle.

Brush the edges of the dough with the beaten egg. Fold the dough over the filling to create a half-moon shape and press the edges together to seal. Place the empanadas on a baking sheet and brush the tops with the remaining beaten egg.

Bake for 15-20 minutes, or until golden brown.

And there you have it, folks. Salmon and Lemon Empanadas that will make your taste buds sing. Serve them up with some lemon wedges or tartar sauce and enjoy. Trust me, these are the real deal. Buen provecho!

Enjoy

14. Shrimp and Bell Pepper Empanadas

Prep: 30 min. Cook: 20 min. Ready In: 50 min. Servings: 4

Ingredients:

1 lb. of raw shrimp, peeled and deveined

1/2 onion, diced

1/2 cup of diced red bell pepper

1/2 cup of diced green bell pepper

1/4 cup of cilantro, chopped

1 teaspoon of cumin

1/2 teaspoon of chili powder

1/2 teaspoon of salt

1/4 teaspoon of black pepper

1/4 cup of grated queso fresco

1 package of store-bought empanada dough

1 egg, beaten

Cooking Directions:

Empanadas, my dear friends, are the ultimate party food. They're easy to make, easy to eat, and can be filled with just about anything. Today, we're going to show you how to make some Shrimp and Bell Pepper Empanadas that will impress your guests and leave them wanting more. Trust me, these empanadas are something special.

In a medium skillet, sauté the onion and bell peppers over medium heat until softened, about 5 minutes. Stir in the shrimp, cilantro, cumin, chili powder, salt, and black pepper. Cook until the shrimp are pink and cooked through, about 5 minutes. Stir in the queso fresco. Cook for a final 2 minutes. Remove from heat and let cool. Preheat the oven to 375 degrees F (190 degrees C). Roll out the store-bought empanada dough on a lightly floured surface. Cut into circles using a cookie cutter or a glass. Place a spoonful of the shrimp and bell pepper mixture on one half of each empanada dough circle. Brush the edges of the dough with the beaten egg. Fold the dough over the filling to create a half-moon shape and press the edges together to seal.

Place the empanadas on a baking sheet and brush the tops with the remaining beaten egg.

Bake for 15-20 minutes, or until golden brown.

And there you have it, folks. Shrimp and Bell Pepper Empanadas that will make your taste buds sing. Serve them up with some salsa or guacamole and enjoy. Trust me, these are the real deal. Buen provecho!

Enjoy

33

15. Tuna and Cucumber Empanadas

Prep: 20 min. Cook: 20 min. Ready In: 40 min. Servings: 4

Ingredients:

All-purpose flour, for dusting

1-pound store-bought empanada dough

1 can (6 ounces) tuna, drained and flaked

1/4 cup diced cucumber

1/4 cup diced red onion

1/4 cup diced red bell pepper

1/4 cup diced green bell pepper

1/4 cup diced jalapeño pepper

2 cloves garlic, minced

1/4 cup chopped fresh cilantro

1/4 cup mayonnaise

1/4 cup sour cream

1/2 teaspoon ground cumin

1/2 teaspoon smoked paprika

1/4 teaspoon salt

1/4 teaspoon black pepper

1 egg, beaten

Cooking Directions:

Empanadas are the ultimate street food, and this tuna and cucumber version is no exception. These flaky, golden-brown pockets of deliciousness are packed with flavor, and are perfect for a quick and easy lunch or dinner. And the best part? You can use store-bought dough, so you don't have to worry about making it from scratch. Let's get started.

Preheat your oven to 375°F (190°C). Line a baking sheet with parchment paper. On a lightly floured surface, roll out the empanada dough to 1/8-inch thickness.

In a medium bowl, combine the tuna, cucumber, red onion, red and green bell peppers, jalapeño, garlic, cilantro, mayonnaise, sour cream, cumin, smoked paprika, salt, and black pepper. Mix well.

Spoon about 2 tablespoons of the tuna mixture onto one half of each dough round, leaving a 1/2-inch border around the edges. Brush the edges with the beaten egg. Fold the dough over the filling, pressing the edges to seal. Crimp the edges with a fork to seal.

Place the empanadas on the prepared baking sheet. Brush the top of each empanada with the beaten egg.

Bake for 20 minutes, or until golden brown.

And there you have it, folks. Tuna and cucumber empanadas that are sure to satisfy. Serve them hot out of the oven and enjoy with a cold beer. Trust me, you won't regret it.

Enjoy

16. Egg and Ham Empanadas

Prep: 15 min. Cook: 30 min. Ready In: 45 min. Servings: 4

Ingredients:

All-purpose flour for dusting

1/2-pound cooked ham, diced

1/4 cup diced onion

1/4 cup diced red bell pepper

1/4 cup diced green bell pepper

2 cloves garlic, minced

1/4 cup chopped fresh cilantro leaves

1 tablespoon olive oil

Salt and ground black pepper to taste

1 cup shredded Monterey Jack cheese

4 large eggs, beaten

1 (15 ounce) package empanada dough or store-bought pie crust

Cooking Directions:

You know, I've always been a fan of empanadas. The flaky crust and the savory filling - it's the perfect combination of textures and flavors. And these egg and ham empanadas, well, they're a classic. They're the perfect party food, or even just a casual lunch. So, grab a beer, and let's get to work.

Preheat oven to 375 degrees F (190 degrees C).

In a large skillet, heat olive oil over medium heat. Add onion, red bell pepper, green bell pepper, and garlic. Cook and stir until vegetables are tender. Stir in cilantro. Season with salt and pepper.

Remove skillet from heat. Stir in ham and shredded cheese. Add beaten eggs and mix well.

Roll out empanada dough on a lightly floured surface to about 1/8-inch thickness. Cut into 4-inch circles.

Place a heaping tablespoon of filling on one half of each circle. Fold dough over filling, and press edges to seal. Crimp edges with a fork to ensure a tight seal.

Place empanadas on a baking sheet.

Bake in the preheated oven for 20 to 25 minutes, or until golden brown.

There you have it folks, perfect egg and ham empanadas. These are best served hot, but they're also great at room temperature. So go ahead, grab one, or two, or three. And as always, enjoy your meal.

Enjoy

17. Chicken and Zucchini Empanadas

Prep: 15 min. Cook: 30 min. Ready In: 45 min. Servings: 4

Ingredients:

All-purpose flour for dusting

1/2-pound cooked chicken, diced

1/2 cup diced zucchini

1/4 cup diced onion

1/4 cup diced red bell pepper

1/4 cup diced green bell pepper

2 cloves garlic, minced

1/4 cup chopped fresh cilantro leaves

1 tablespoon olive oil

Salt and ground black pepper to taste

1 cup shredded Monterey Jack cheese

4 large eggs, beaten

1 (15 ounce) package empanada dough or store-bought pie crust

Cooking Directions:

Empanadas, empanadas, empanadas. I can't get enough of these tasty little pockets of goodness. And these chicken and zucchini empanadas, they're something special. The combination of tender chicken and fresh zucchini is just fantastic. So, fire up the oven and let's get to work.

Preheat oven to 375 degrees F (190 degrees C).

In a large skillet, heat olive oil over medium heat. Add onion, red bell pepper, green bell pepper, and garlic. Cook and stir until vegetables are tender. Stir in cilantro. Season with salt and pepper.

Remove skillet from heat. Stir in chicken and shredded cheese. Add beaten eggs and mix well.

Roll out empanada dough on a lightly floured surface to about 1/8-inch thickness. Cut into 4-inch circles.

Place a heaping tablespoon of filling on one half of each circle. Fold dough over filling, and press edges to seal. Crimp edges with a fork to ensure a tight seal.

Place empanadas on a baking sheet.

Bake in the preheated oven for 20 to 25 minutes, or until golden brown.

And there you have it folks, chicken and zucchini empanadas. These are best served hot, but they're also great at room temperature. So go ahead, grab one, or two, or three. And as always, enjoy your meal.

Enjoy

18. Pork and Blue Berry Empanadas

Prep: 15 min. Cook: 30 min. Ready In: 45 min. Servings: 4

Ingredients:

All-purpose flour for dusting

1/2-pound cooked pork, diced

1/4 cup diced onion

1/4 cup diced red bell pepper

1/4 cup diced green bell pepper

1/2 cup fresh blueberries

2 cloves garlic, minced

1/4 cup chopped fresh cilantro leaves

1 tablespoon olive oil

Salt and ground black pepper to taste

1 cup shredded Monterey Jack cheese

4 large eggs, beaten

1 (15 ounce) package empanada dough or store-bought pie crust

Cooking Directions:

Empanadas, empanadas, empanadas. I love empanadas. The flaky crust, the savory filling. And these pork and blueberry empanadas, well they're something special. The sweetness of the blueberries and the savory pork, it's a unique and delicious combination. So, fire up the oven and let's get to work.

Preheat oven to 375 degrees F (190 degrees C).

In a large skillet, heat olive oil over medium heat. Add onion, red bell pepper, green bell pepper, and garlic. Cook and stir until vegetables are tender. Stir in cilantro. Season with salt and pepper.

Remove skillet from heat. Stir in pork, blueberries, and shredded cheese. Add beaten eggs and mix well.

Roll out empanada dough on a lightly floured surface to about 1/8-inch thickness. Cut into 4-inch circles.

Place a heaping tablespoon of filling on one half of each circle. Fold dough over filling, and press edges to seal. Crimp edges with a fork to ensure a tight seal.

Place empanadas on a baking sheet.

Bake in the preheated oven for 20 to 25 minutes, or until golden brown.

And there you have it folks, pork and blueberry empanadas. Although it's not a traditional combination of ingredients, it's a unique and delicious flavor. These are best served hot, but they're also great at room temperature. So go ahead, grab one, or two, or three. And as always, enjoy your meal.

Enjoy

19. Black Beans and Sweet Pepper Empanadas

Prep: 15 min. Cook: 30 min. Ready In: 45 min. Servings: 4

Ingredients:

All-purpose flour for dusting

1 (15 ounce) can black beans, drained and rinsed

1/4 cup diced onion

1/4 cup diced red bell pepper

1/4 cup diced green bell pepper

1/4 cup diced sweet pepper

2 cloves garlic, minced

1/4 cup chopped fresh cilantro leaves

1 tablespoon olive oil

Salt and ground black pepper to taste

1 cup shredded Monterey Jack cheese

4 large eggs, beaten

1 (15 ounce) package empanada dough or store-bought pie crust

Cooking Directions:

Empanadas, empanadas, empanadas. I've had my fair share of these delicious pockets of goodness, and I've got to say, these black bean and sweet pepper empanadas are something special. The combination of savory black beans and sweet peppers is a classic and always a crowd pleaser. So, let's get to work and make some empanadas.

Preheat oven to 375 degrees F (190 degrees C).

In a large skillet, heat olive oil over medium heat. Add onion, red bell pepper, green bell pepper, sweet pepper, and garlic. Cook and stir until vegetables are tender. Stir in cilantro. Season with salt and pepper.

Remove skillet from heat. Stir in black beans and shredded cheese. Add beaten eggs and mix well.

Roll out empanada dough on a lightly floured surface to about 1/8-inch thickness. Cut into 4-inch circles.

Place a heaping tablespoon of filling on one half of each circle. Fold dough over filling, and press edges to seal. Crimp edges with a fork to ensure a tight seal.

Place empanadas on a baking sheet.

Bake in the preheated oven for 20 to 25 minutes, or until golden brown.

And there you have it folks, black bean and sweet pepper empanadas that are sure to be a hit at any gathering. These are best served hot, but they're also great at room temperature. So go ahead, grab one, or two, or three. And as always, enjoy your meal.

Enjoy

20. Shrimp and Garlic Empanadas

Prep: 15 min. Cook: 30 min. Ready In: 45 min. Servings: 4

Ingredients:

All-purpose flour for dusting

1/2-pound cooked shrimp, peeled and deveined

1/4 cup diced onion

1/4 cup diced red bell pepper

1/4 cup diced green bell pepper

2 cloves garlic, minced

1/4 cup chopped fresh cilantro leaves

1 tablespoon olive oil

Salt and ground black pepper to taste

1 cup shredded Monterey Jack cheese

4 large eggs, beaten

1 (15 ounce) package empanada dough or store-bought pie crust

Cooking Directions:

Empanadas, empanadas, empanadas. I've had my fair share of these delicious pockets of goodness, and let me tell you, these shrimp and garlic empanadas are something special. The combination of succulent shrimp and fragrant garlic is a match made in heaven. So, let's get to work and make some empanadas.

Preheat oven to 375 degrees F (190 degrees C).

In a large skillet, heat olive oil over medium heat. Add onion, red bell pepper, green bell pepper and garlic. Cook and stir until vegetables are tender. Stir in cilantro. Season with salt and pepper.

Remove skillet from heat. Stir in shrimp and shredded cheese. Add beaten eggs and mix well.

Roll out empanada dough on a lightly floured surface to about 1/8-inch thickness. Cut into 4-inch circles.

Place a heaping tablespoon of filling on one half of each circle. Fold dough over filling, and press edges to seal. Crimp edges with a fork to ensure a tight seal.

Place empanadas on a baking sheet.

Bake in the preheated oven for 20 to 25 minutes, or until golden brown.

And there you have it folks, shrimp and garlic empanadas that are sure to be a hit at any gathering. These are best served hot, but they're also great at room temperature. So go ahead, grab one, or two, or three. And as always, enjoy your meal.

Enjoy

21. Beef, Olive and Raisin Empanadas

Prep: 20 min. Cook: 25 min. Ready in: 45 min. Servings: 4

Ingredients:

Store-bought empanada dough (12 discs)

1 tablespoon olive oil

1/2 pound ground beef

1/2 cup finely chopped onion

2 garlic cloves, minced

1/2 teaspoon ground cumin

1/2 teaspoon paprika

1/4 teaspoon salt

1/4 teaspoon black pepper

1/4 cup finely chopped green olives

1/4 cup raisins

1 egg, beaten (for egg wash)

Cooking Directions:

Embark on a culinary adventure with these Beef, Olive, and Raisin Empanadas. The delightful blend of savory ground beef, tangy green olives, and sweet raisins creates a unique treat that's perfect for any mealtime occasion. Whether you serve them as a tempting appetizer or a satisfying main course, these empanadas are sure to delight.

In a large skillet, heat the olive oil over medium heat. Add the ground beef and cook, breaking it up with a spoon, for 5 to 7 minutes, or until browned and cooked through.

Add the chopped onion and minced garlic to the skillet and cook, stirring occasionally, for 3 to 5 minutes, or until the onion is softened and slightly translucent.

Stir in the ground cumin, paprika, salt, and black pepper, cooking for an additional minute.

Remove the skillet from the heat and stir in the chopped green olives and raisins, mixing well to combine.

Preheat your oven to 400°F (200°C) and line a baking sheet with parchment paper.

Roll out the store-bought empanada dough and cut out circles about 5 inches in diameter. You can use a round cookie cutter or an appropriately sized bowl as a guide.

Place a spoonful of the beef, olive, and raisin filling in the center of each dough circle.

Fold the dough over the filling, creating a half-moon shape, and press the edges together with your fingers to seal. You can use a fork to create a decorative pattern around the edges if you'd like.

Arrange the filled empanadas on the prepared baking sheet. Brush the tops with the beaten egg to give them a gorgeous golden sheen.

Bake the empanadas for 20 to 25 minutes, or until they're golden brown and crispy. Allow them to cool for a few minutes before serving.

Enjoy

22. Tuna and Red Pepper Empanadas

Prep: 20 min. Cook: 20 min. Ready in: 40 min. Servings: 4

Ingredients:

4 pie crusts

2 cans of tuna, drained

1 red bell pepper, diced

1/4 cup diced onion

1 clove garlic, minced

1 tsp dried oregano

Salt and pepper to taste

1 egg, beaten

2 tbsp olive oil

Cooking Directions:

Alright folks, grab your aprons and let's get cookin'! Today, we're making Tuna and Red Pepper Empanadas, a flavorful and hearty dish that's perfect for lunch or dinner. With store-bought pie crust dough and a few simple ingredients, we're going to create a dish that's easy to make and absolutely delicious.

Alright, let's start by preheating our oven to 400°F.

In a pan, we're going to heat up some olive oil over medium heat, and then add in some minced garlic, diced onion, and diced red bell pepper. Cook until those veggies are nice and soft, about 5 minutes.

Next, we'll add in our drained tuna, along with some dried oregano, and some salt and pepper to taste. Cook for another 2-3 minutes, until everything is well combined. And then, remove from heat and let it cool.

We're gonna take our store-bought pie crust and cut it into 4 equal pieces. Roll each piece into a circle, about 7-8 inches in diameter.

Spoon some of the tuna mixture onto one half of each pie crust circle, leaving about a half inch of space around the edges. Brush the edges with a beaten egg, and then fold the other half of the pie crust over the filling, pressing the edges together to seal.

Place the empanadas on a baking sheet lined with parchment paper, and brush the top of each empanada with the remaining beaten egg.

Pop 'em in the oven and bake for 15-20 minutes, or until the crust is nice and golden brown.

And there you have it, folks! Tuna and Red Pepper Empanadas that are easy to make and packed with flavor. Serve hot with your favorite dipping sauce on the side.

Enjoy

23. Egg and Sausage Empanadas

Prep: 20 min. Cook: 20 min. Ready in: 40 min. Servings: 4

Ingredients:

4 pie crusts

4 eggs

1/2 lb. breakfast sausage, crumbled and cooked

1/4 cup diced onion

1/4 cup diced red bell pepper

1 clove garlic, minced

Salt and pepper to taste

1 egg, beaten

2 tbsp olive oil

Cooking Directions:

Alright folks, it's time to get our brunch on with our next dish! Today, we're making Egg and Sausage Empanadas, a savory and satisfying meal that's perfect for breakfast or brunch. With store-bought pie crust dough and a few simple ingredients, we're going to create a dish that's easy to make and oh-so delicious.

Alright, let's start by preheating our oven to 400°F.

In a pan, we're going to heat up some olive oil over medium heat, and then add in some minced garlic, diced onion, and diced red bell pepper. Cook until those veggies are nice and soft, about 5 minutes.

Next, in a separate pan, we'll scramble our eggs until they're cooked. And then, remove from heat and let it cool.

We're gonna take our store-bought pie crust and cut it into 4 equal pieces. Roll each piece into a circle, about 7-8 inches in diameter.

Spoon some of the crumbled and cooked sausage, eggs, and veggies onto one half of each pie crust circle, leaving about a half inch of space around the edges. Brush the edges with a beaten egg, and then fold the other half of the pie crust over the filling, pressing the edges together to seal.

Place the empanadas on a baking sheet lined with parchment paper, and brush the top of each empanada with the remaining beaten egg.

Pop 'em in the oven and bake for 15-20 minutes, or until the crust is nice and golden brown.

And there you have it, folks! Egg and Sausage Empanadas that are easy to make and loaded with flavor. Perfect for a lazy Sunday brunch or a quick and easy breakfast. Serve with a cup of coffee and you're good to go.

Enjoy

24. Turkey and Stuffing Empanadas

Prep: 15 min. Cook: 25 min. Ready in: 40 min. Servings: 4

Ingredients:

1/2 cup diced onion

1/2 cup diced celery

2 cloves garlic, minced

1 1/2 cups chopped cooked turkey

1 cup prepared stuffing

1/2 cup cranberry sauce

Salt and pepper, to taste

1 egg, lightly beaten

2 tablespoons water

2 (9-inch) rounds store-bought pie dough

Cooking Directions:

Now, let's get cooking! Empanadas are a classic dish from South America and are basically turnovers filled with all sorts of tasty ingredients. Today, we're making a twist on the traditional recipe by filling our empanadas with a combination of juicy turkey, savory stuffing, and tangy cranberry sauce.

To start, let's make the filling. In a skillet over medium heat, sauté the onion, celery, and garlic until softened, about 5 minutes. Add the turkey and stuffing and continue to cook for an additional 2-3 minutes, stirring occasionally. Stir in the cranberry sauce, season with salt and pepper to taste, and set aside to cool.

Next, let's assemble the empanadas. Preheat your oven to 375°F (190°C). Roll out the pie dough on a lightly floured surface to about 1/8 inch thick. Cut the dough into 4 equal pieces.

Place about 1/4 of the filling in the center of each piece of dough. Brush the edges of the dough with the beaten egg and water mixture. Fold the dough over the filling to form a half-moon shape, pressing the edges together to seal. Cut a few slits in the top of each empanada to allow steam to escape.

Bake the empanadas on a baking sheet for 25 minutes or until golden brown. Serve hot and…

Enjoy

25. Beef and Green Olive Empanadas

Prep: 30 min. Cook: 20 min. Ready in: 50 min. Servings: 4

Ingredients:

1 pound ground beef

1/2 cup diced onion

1/2 cup diced green olives

1/2 teaspoon dried oregano

1/2 teaspoon ground cumin

1/2 teaspoon paprika

1/2 teaspoon salt

1/4 teaspoon black pepper

1 tablespoon olive oil

1 package of empanada dough

1 egg, beaten

Cooking Directions:

Empanadas, the perfect handheld comfort food. They're crispy, flaky, and packed with flavor. And these Beef and Green Olive Empanadas are no exception. They are the perfect way to use up any leftover ground beef you might have, and the green olives add a delicious briny twist to this classic dish.

To start, heat the olive oil in a large skillet over medium heat. Add the onion and cook until soft and translucent, about 5 minutes. Then, add the ground beef and cook until browned, about 7-8 minutes. Stir in the green olives, oregano, cumin, paprika, salt, and pepper, and cook for another 2-3 minutes. Set aside to cool.

Next, preheat your oven to 375°F and line a baking sheet with parchment paper. Roll out the empanada dough on a lightly floured surface to 1/8-inch thickness. Cut the dough into 4-inch rounds. Spoon about 2 tablespoons of the beef filling onto one half of each round, leaving a 1/2-inch border around the edges. Brush the edges with the beaten egg and fold the other half of the dough over the filling, pressing the edges to seal. Place the empanadas on the prepared baking sheet and brush the tops with the remaining egg.

Bake the empanadas for 20-25 minutes, or until they're golden brown and crispy. Serve warm and...

Enjoy

26. Pork and Apple Empanadas

Prep: 30 min. Cook: 20 min. Ready in: 50 min. Servings: 4

Ingredients:

1 pound ground pork

1 large Granny Smith apple, peeled, cored, and diced

1/2 cup diced onion

1/2 teaspoon dried thyme

1/2 teaspoon salt

1/4 teaspoon black pepper

1 tablespoon olive oil

1 package of empanada dough

1 egg, beaten

Cooking Directions:

Ah, the humble empanada, a staple in kitchens all over the world. Each bite of these Pork and Apple Empanadas is a flavor explosion, with juicy ground pork and sweet, tart apples nestled inside a flaky, golden crust. So, let's get cooking, shall we?

To start, heat the olive oil in a large skillet over medium heat. Add the onion and cook until soft and translucent, about 5 minutes. Then, add the ground pork and cook until browned, about 7-8 minutes. Stir in the apples, thyme, salt, and pepper, and cook for another 2-3 minutes. Set aside to cool.

Next, preheat your oven to 375°F and line a baking sheet with parchment paper. Roll out the empanada dough on a lightly floured surface to 1/8-inch thickness. Cut the dough into 4-inch rounds. Spoon about 2 tablespoons of the pork and apple filling onto one half of each round, leaving a 1/2-inch border around the edges. Brush the edges with the beaten egg and fold the other half of the dough over the filling, pressing the edges to seal. Place the empanadas on the prepared baking sheet and brush the tops with the remaining egg.

Bake the empanadas for 20-25 minutes, or until they're golden brown and crispy. Serve warm and...

Enjoy

27. Pork and Cabbage Empanadas

Prep: 30 min. Cook: 20 min. Ready in: 50 min. Servings: 4

Ingredients:

1 pound ground pork

1/2 cup diced onion

1/2 cup shredded cabbage

1/2 teaspoon dried thyme

1/2 teaspoon salt

1/4 teaspoon black pepper

1 tablespoon olive oil

1 package of empanada dough

1 egg, beaten

Cooking Directions:

Ladies and gentlemen, gather around, because I've got a treat for you. These Pork and Cabbage Empanadas are the stuff of legends. The juicy ground pork and crisp cabbage, encased in a flaky, golden crust, are sure to tantalize your taste buds and leave you coming back for more. So let's dive in, shall we?

To start, heat the olive oil in a large skillet over medium heat. Add the onion and cook until soft and translucent, about 5 minutes. Then, add the ground pork and cook until browned, about 7-8 minutes. Stir in the cabbage, thyme, salt, and pepper, and cook for another 2-3 minutes. Set aside to cool.

Next, preheat your oven to 375°F and line a baking sheet with parchment paper. Roll out the empanada dough on a lightly floured surface to 1/8-inch thickness. Cut the dough into 4-inch rounds. Spoon about 2 tablespoons of the pork and cabbage filling onto one half of each round, leaving a 1/2-inch border around the edges. Brush the edges with the beaten egg and fold the other half of the dough over the filling, pressing the edges to seal. Place the empanadas on the prepared baking sheet and brush the tops with the remaining egg.

And there you have it, folks! These Pork and Cabbage Empanadas are the perfect way to enjoy a comforting, flavorful meal. So go ahead, grab one (or two, we won't judge), sit back, and savor each bite. These empanadas are the epitome of handheld heaven.

Enjoy

28. Chicken and Red Pepper Empanadas

Prep: 30 min. Cook: 20 min. Ready in: 50 min. Servings: 4

Ingredients:

1 pound boneless, skinless chicken breast, cooked and diced

1 red bell pepper, diced

1/2 cup diced onion

1/2 teaspoon dried basil

1/2 teaspoon salt

1/4 teaspoon black pepper

1 tablespoon olive oil

1 package of empanada dough

1 egg, beaten

Cooking Directions:

Ladies and gentlemen, gather around for a flavor experience like no other! These Chicken and Red Pepper Empanadas are the epitome of handheld heaven, with juicy chicken and crisp red bell pepper nestled inside a flaky, golden crust. So, let's get cooking!

To start, heat the olive oil in a large skillet over medium heat. Add the onion and cook until soft and translucent, about 5 minutes. Then, add the diced chicken and red bell pepper and cook for another 2-3 minutes. Stir in the basil, salt, and pepper, and cook for another minute. Set aside to cool.

Next, preheat your oven to 375°F and line a baking sheet with parchment paper. Roll out the empanada dough on a lightly floured surface to 1/8-inch thickness. Cut the dough into 4-inch rounds. Spoon about 2 tablespoons of the chicken and red pepper filling onto one half of each round, leaving a 1/2-inch border around the edges. Brush the edges with the beaten egg and fold the other half of the dough over the filling, pressing the edges to seal. Place the empanadas on the prepared baking sheet and brush the tops with the remaining egg.

Bake the empanadas for 20-25 minutes, or until they're golden brown and crispy.

And there you have it folks, the star of the show, the Chicken and Red Pepper Empanadas. Each flaky bite is a celebration of flavor, with juicy chicken and crisp red bell pepper taking center stage. So go ahead, grab a bite and let the good times roll!

Enjoy

29. Salmon and Garlic Empanadas

Prep: 30 min. Cook: 20 min. Ready in: 50 min. Servings: 4

Ingredients:

1 pound salmon, cooked and flaked

1/2 cup diced onion

2 cloves garlic, minced

1/2 teaspoon dried dill

1/2 teaspoon salt

1/4 teaspoon black pepper

1 tablespoon olive oil

1 package of empanada dough

1 egg, beaten

Cooking Directions:

Ladies and gentlemen, hold onto your taste buds! These Salmon and Garlic Empanadas are about to take you on a flavor journey like no other. The juicy salmon and pungent garlic are nestled inside a flaky, golden crust, making each bite a true delight.

To start, heat the olive oil in a large skillet over medium heat. Add the onion and cook until soft and translucent, about 5 minutes. Then, add the garlic and cook for another minute. Stir in the salmon, dill, salt, and pepper, and cook for another 2-3 minutes. Set aside to cool.

Next, preheat your oven to 375°F and line a baking sheet with parchment paper. Roll out the empanada dough on a lightly floured surface to 1/8-inch thickness. Cut the dough into 4-inch rounds. Spoon about 2 tablespoons of the salmon and garlic filling onto one half of each round, leaving a 1/2-inch border around the edges. Brush the edges with the beaten egg and fold the other half of the dough over the filling, pressing the edges to seal. Place the empanadas on the prepared baking sheet and brush the tops with the remaining egg.

Bake the empanadas for 20-25 minutes, or until they're golden brown and crispy.

And there you have it folks, the salmon sensation, the Garlic and Salmon Empanadas. Each flaky bite is a celebration of the sea, with juicy salmon and pungent garlic taking center stage. So go ahead, grab a bite and let the waves of flavor wash over you!

Enjoy

30. Shrimp and Ginger Empanadas

Prep: 30 min. Cook: 20 min. Ready in: 50 min. Servings: 4

Ingredients:

1 pound shrimp, cooked and peeled

1/2 cup diced onion

1 tablespoon grated fresh ginger

1/2 teaspoon dried basil

1/2 teaspoon salt

1/4 teaspoon black pepper

1 tablespoon olive oil

1 package of empanada dough

1 egg, beaten

Cooking Directions:

Ladies and gentlemen, gather around for a flavor explosion like no other! These Shrimp and Ginger Empanadas are the perfect blend of sweet and spicy, with juicy shrimp and zesty ginger encased in a flaky, golden crust.

To start, heat the olive oil in a large skillet over medium heat. Add the onion and cook until soft and translucent, about 5 minutes. Then, add the ginger and cook for another minute. Stir in the shrimp, basil, salt, and pepper, and cook for another 2-3 minutes. Set aside to cool.

Next, preheat your oven to 375°F and line a baking sheet with parchment paper. Roll out the empanada dough on a lightly floured surface to 1/8-inch thickness. Cut the dough into 4-inch rounds. Spoon about 2 tablespoons of the shrimp and ginger filling onto one half of each round, leaving a 1/2-inch border around the edges. Brush the edges with the beaten egg and fold the other half of the dough over the filling, pressing the edges to seal. Place the empanadas on the prepared baking sheet and brush the tops with the remaining egg.

Bake the empanadas for 20-25 minutes, or until they're golden brown and crispy.

And there you have it folks, the flavor fiesta, the Shrimp and Ginger Empanadas. Each flaky bite is a whirlwind of flavor, with juicy shrimp and zesty ginger taking center stage. So go ahead, grab a bite and let the good times roll!

Enjoy

Thank you for purchasing
Top 30 Most Delicious Empanada Recipes.

We hope you found the recipes as tasteful and delicious as we do.

Please show your support and love for empanadas by leaving a review on Amazon.

Make sure to check out all the other delicious recipes in the Top 30 Most Delicious cookbook series.

Printed in Great Britain
by Amazon

28649508R10040